TIM WHITE
MIRROR OF DREAMS

NORMA
Editorial

MIRROR OF DREAMS
Tim White
First edition: October, 1994
NORMA Editorial, S.A.
Passeig de Sant Joan, 7, pral. 08010 Barcelona (Spain)
Tel. (93) 232 62 12 • Fax int. (343) 231 26 99
© 1994 Tim White
© 1994 NORMA Editorial, S.A. for this edition
Spanish translation by Mercè Caba
German translation by Sabine Schwenk
French translation by Scotch Arleston
All rights reserved
Co-edition & production handled by NORMA Editorial, S.A.
D.L.: B-30308-94
ISBN: 84-7904-243-5
Printed in Spain by INDICE, S.L.

ALL THINGS ARE POSSIBLE

There is no barrier, or frontier, or place in time or space that cannot be reached by imagination. The world of mankind is the product of imagination. But this creative energy is a double - edged sword - it can be our saviour or destroyer. Imagination has created medical science, which has saved countless millions. It has also created weapons of horrifying power such as the atomic bomb, which threaten all life on our planet. Science - the true product of imagination - has sent machines into space, even beyond our solar system, and viewed the distant horizons of the universe, giving us a better understanding of the real vastness and awesome power of the mysterious cosmos. This is an impressive achievement for a creature who's tenure on this world is so comparitively short. But mistakes are many - as environmental damage and so many wars attest. Mankind does not fully understand itself. In fact, the workings of the mind are as mysterious as the cosmos itself. The human brain is a kind of computer, divided into two halves. Two halves that, to all intents and purposes, remain independent of each other - yet are linked. One hemisphere controls the logical, consoious mind; the other drives the more intuitive and creative subcionscious mind - the place we visit when we sleep and dream. It is this subconscious world that is the forge of creativity. The conscious mind assimilates this raw, creative force into ideas.

Who can doubt the mysterious power of imagination? To demonstrate its power - the power within you - try a simple experiment. DON'T THINK OF A RED CAT WHIT GREEN EYES! The chances are, you just saw one! Being a creature of free will and spirit, the world DON'T guaranteed you DID. In an instant your imagination created the image, even though such a creature does not exist in our world. Such is the power of your imagination!

This kind of creative visualisation is employed by artist, especially those, such as fantasy artist, whose works is almost totally imaginative, breaching the barriers of perceived reality. Tim White is one of these artists. His work explores the hidden worlds of possibility, reflecting the light and reflecting the dark - a mirror of dreams.

TODO ES POSIBLE

No existe ninguna barrera ni frontera ni lugar en el tiempo o el espacio que no puedan ser alcanzados por la imaginación. El mundo de la humanidad es producto de la imaginación. Pero esta energía creativa es un arma de doble filo, puede salvarnos o destruirnos. La imaginación ha creado la ciencia médica que ha salvado a millones de personas. Pero también ha creado armas de potencia tan terrorífica como la bomba atómica, que amenazan toda la vida que pueda existir en el planeta. La ciencia, auténtico producto de la imaginación, ha posibilitado el lanzamiento de máquinas al espacio, incluso más allá de nuestro sistema solar, y ha podido divisar los lejanos horizontes del universo lo cual ha propiciado una mejor comprensión de la verdadera enormidad y del admirable poder del misterioso cosmos. Éste es un logro impresionante para una criatura cuyo paso por este mundo es, comparativamente, tan corto.
Pero hay muchos errores tal como demuestran los datos medioambientales y las muchas guerras. La humanidad no se comprende del todo a sí misma. De hecho, los procesos mentales son tan misteriosos como el propio cosmos. El cerebro humano es una especie de ordenador dividido en dos mitades. Dos mitades que permanecen independientes una de otra, aun cuando están relacionadas. Un hemisferio controla la mente lógica y consciente; el otro rige el subconsciente, más intuitivo y creativo, el lugar que visitamos cuando dormimos y soñamos. Este mundo subconsciente es la forja de la creatividad. La mente consciente asimila dicha fuerza creativa puliéndola y convirtiéndola en ideas.

¿Quién duda del misterioso poder de la imaginación? Para demostrar su poder, el poder que existe dentro de usted mismo, haga un sencillo experimento. ¡NO PIENSE EN UN GATO ROJO CON OJOS VERDES! ¡Seguro que acaba usted de visualizarlo! Como ser humano libre, de voluntad y de espíritu, el mandato NO PIENSE ha garantizado lo que usted PENSARA puesto que es usted y nadie más quien controla su mente. En unos breves instantes su mente ha creado una imagen como la descrita aunque una criatura así no exista en nuestro mundo. ¡Hasta tal punto llega el poder de nuestra imaginación!

Este tipo de visualización creativa es la empleada por los ilustradores, especialmente por aquellos ilustradores de fantasía cuya obra es casi totalmente producto de la imaginación, una obra que transgrede la barrera de la percepción de la realidad. Tim White es uno de ellos. Su obra explora los mundos ocultos de lo posible reflejando la luz y la oscuridad, y es, en definitiva, un Espejo de los Sueños.

ALLES IST MÖGLICH

Es gibt keine Schranken, keine Grenzen und keinen Ort in Raum und Zeit, den wir mit unserer Phantasie nicht erreichen könnten. Die Welt der Menschen ist ein Produkt der Vorstellungskraft. Aber diese kreative Energie ist eine zweischneidige Sache - sie kann uns Heil oder Zerstörung bringen. Die Phantasie hat die Medizin hervorgebracht, durch die Millionen und Abermillionen von Menschen gerettet wurden. Sie hat aber auch Waffen hervorgebracht wie die Atombombe, deren schreckenerregende Kraft alles Leben auf unserem Planeten bedroht. Die Wissenschaft, das eigentliche Produkt der Phantasie, hat es uns ermöglicht, Maschinen in den Weltraum, ja sogar jenseits unseres Sonnensystems zu schicken und einen Blick auf die entferntesten Horizonte des Universums zu werfen. Das hilft uns, die ungeheuren Ausmaße und die ehrfurchtgebietende Gewalt des mysteriösen Kosmos zu erfassen. Dies alles sind beeindruckende Leistungen für ein Wesen, dessen Zeit auf dieser Erde vergleichsweise kurz ist. Aber es werden auch viele Fehler gemacht–das beweisen Umweltzerstörung und Krieg. Der Mensch hat sich selbst noch nicht ganz verstanden. Im Grunde ist uns der Verstand ebenso rätselhaft geblieben wie der Kosmos. Das menschliche Gehirn ist eine Art Computer, der sich in zwei Hälften teilt. Zwei Hälften, die unabhängig voneinander bleiben und doch miteinander verbunden sind. Die eine Hemisphäre kontrolliert das logische, bewußte Denken; die andere lenkt das intuitivere und kreativere unterbewußte Denken–den Ort, an dem wir uns befinden, wenn wir schlafen und träumen. Diese unterbewußte Welt ist die Schmiede der Kreativität. Das bewußte Denken lenkt die zunächst rohe kreative Energie in die Welt der Ideen.

Wer könnte die geheimnisvolle Macht der Phantasie bezweifeln? Um diese Macht, die auch in Ihnen steckt, zu demonstrieren, versuchen Sie ein kleines Experiment. DENKEN SIE NICHT AN EINE ROTE KATZE MIT GRÜNEN AUGEN! Wahrscheinlich haben Sie gerade eine gesehen! Da Sie ein Wesen sind, das über einen freien Willen und einen freien Geist verfügt, hat die Aufforderung DENKEN SIE NICHT garantiert dafür gesorgt, daß Sie es doch taten. Denn Sie selbst kontrollieren ihr Denken, niemand anders. Ihre Vorstellungskraft hat sofort das Bild erzeugt, obwohl es so ein Wesen in unserer Welt überhaupt nicht gibt. So mächtig ist Ihre Phantasie!

Diese kreative, visuelle Kraft wird von Künstlern benutzt, besonders von solchen, die wie die Fantasy-Künstler ausschließlich im Bereich der Phantasie arbeiten und die Grenzen der wahrnehmbaren Realität durchbrechen. Tim White zählt zu diesen Künstlern. Mit seiner Arbeit erforscht er die versteckte Welt des Möglichen, in der sich Licht und Dunkelheit reflektieren–wie in einem Spiegel der Träume...

TOUT EST POSSIBLE

Il n'y a pas de barrière, de frontière, de lieu, dans le temps ou dans l'espace, qui ne puisse être atteint par l'imagination. Le monde des hommes lui-même a été façonné par notre imagination. Mais cette énergie créatrice est comme une épée tranchante à double lame: elle peut nous sauver ou nous détruire. L'imagination a créé la science de la médecine, qui sauve des milliers d'hommes. Mais elle a aussi engendré des armes d'un pouvoir terrifiant: la bombe atomique menace la vie de notre planète.

La science, pure prolongation de l'imagination, a envoyé des machines à travers l'espace, parfois même au-delà de notre système solaire. Grâce à elle, nous pouvons contempler les lointains horizons de l'univers, mieux comprendre l'infiniment grand, nous approcher des terrifiants pouvoirs du mystérieux cosmos. C'est un exploit impressionnant pour une créature, l'homme qui est comparativement depuis si peu de temps sur terre. Mais les erreurs sont nombreuses, comme les ravages causés à l'environnement, et les multiples guerres le prouvent.

L'homme semble ne pas se comprendre lui-même. En réalité, le fonctionnement de l'esprit est aussi mystérieux que le cosmos. Le cerveau humain est une sorte d'ordinateur divisé en deux moitiés. Celles-ci, bien qu'enchaînées l'une à l'autre, restent indépendantes dans leur fonctionnement et leur utilité. Un hémisphère contrôle la logique, l'esprit conscient. L'autre dirige la partie la plus intuitive, créative, l'esprit subconscient. C'est le lieu que nous visitons lorsque nous dormons et rêvons, c'est le berceau de la créativité. L'esprit conscient assimile un matériau brut, la réalité, et les forces créatives du subconscient transforment ce matériau en idées.

Qui peut douter du mystérieux pouvoir de l'imagination? Pour montrer que sa puissance est en chacun de vous, tentez une expérience simple: NE PENSEZ PAS à un chat rouge avec des yeux verts! Eh bien oui, vous venez tout de même d'en voir un. Votre esprit a sa propre volonté : il suffit de vous dire NE PENSEZ PAS A pour que vous le fassiez ! En un instant, vous avez créé l'image d'un être qui n'existe pas dans notre monde. Tel est le pouvoir de votre imagination!

Ce type de visualisation créative est employé par les artistes. Particulièrement ceux, comme les dessinateurs de fantastique, qui travaillent sur un matériau à presque complètement imaginaire et renversent les réalités de la réalité perceptible. Tim White est l'un de ces artistes. Ses travaux explorent les mondes cachés du possible, reflètent la lumière ou les ténèbres comme un miroir des rêves.

Dark Side of The Sun

A surveillance device, micro-engineered into the form of a mosquito: it has cameras, listening gear, and offensive capabilities. Because of its small size and power of flight it can get past through the most security precautions. This was taken from a pen and ink drawing that already existed and coincided with the plot of the book. For the roughs the artist used a photo-print of the drawing cut out on a background, then he coloured everything with felt tip pens. The cup ring mark is courtesy of the then art department of the New English Library!

Eine Überwachungsvorrichtung in der winzigen Gestalt einer Mücke verfügt über Kameras, Abhörgeräte und über ein Angriffspotential. Durch ihre geringe Größe und ihre Flugkraft ist sie in der Lage, die meisten Sicherheitsanlagen zu passieren. Das Bild geht auf eine Tuschezeichnung zurück, die bereits existierte und zur Handlung des Buches paßte. Für die Entwürfe benutzte der Künstler einen Photoabzug der Zeichnung, die er ausschnitt und dann das Ganze mit Filzstiften kolorierte. Ein besonderer Dank gilt der damaligen Kunstabteilung der New English Library für den hinterlassenen Kaffeering!

Se trata de un instrumento de vigilancia construido mediante microingeniería con forma de mosquito: está dotado de cámaras, aparatos de audición y otras opciones. Gracias a su pequeño tamaño y a su capacidad de volar puede pasar inadvertido para la mayoría de medidas de seguridad. Esta ilustración fue tomada de un dibujo a lápiz y tinta que ya existía y que coincidía con el argumento del libro.Para los bocetos, el ilustrador empleó una fotografía del dibujo recortado de su fondo y luego lo coloreó todo con rotuladores. La marca de la taza es una cortesía del entonces departamento artístico de la New English Library.

Un dispositif de surveillance, miniaturisé sous forme de moustique. Il a des caméras, un équipement audio et des capacités offensives. Du fait de sa petite taille et de son adresse en vol, il peut se glisser au travers des dispositifs de sécurité les plus sophistiqués. C'est une partie d'un dessin au crayon et à l'encre réalisé précédemment et qui coïncidait avec l'intrigue du livre. Pour les esquisses, le dessinateur a utilisé un tirage photo du dessin, découpé un fond, puis il a effectué la mise en couleurs de l'ensemble au stylo feutre. La marque laissée par une tasse est là grâce à l'aimable participation du département artistique de la New English Library !

Forest of the Night

A young boy's older brother has been abducted and taken into another dimension by the king of the forces of darkness. The young boy secretly gains access in a bid to rescue his brother, but becomes lost and is befriended by a giant leopard-like creature who acts as a guide. Together they travel through the mysterious, dream-like world with its enchanting landscapes and glowing waterfalls, secking to reclaim his brother from the dark forces that have taken him.

El hermano mayor de un niño ha sido raptado y llevado a otra dimensión por el rey de las fuerzas de la oscuridad. El niño, en una apuesta secreta, gana el acceso al rescate de su hermano pero se pierde y hace amistad con una criatura gigantesca parecida a un leopardo que le sirve de guía. Viajan juntos a través de un misterioso mundo de ensueño con encantadores paisajes y resplandecientes cascadas en el intento de rescatar a su hermano de las oscuras fuerzas que le tienen prisionero.

Der ältere Bruder eines kleinen Jungen ist vom König der dunklen Gewalten entführt und in eine andere Dimension gebracht worden. Dem kleinen Jungen gelingt es auf Anhieb, dorthin zu gelangen, um seinen Bruder zu retten, aber er verirrt sich und wird von einem riesigen, leopardenartigen Geschöpf aufgenommen, das sich ihm zum Führer macht. Gemeinsam reisen sie durch die geheimnisvolle, traumhafte Welt mit ihren zauberhaften Landschaften und leuchtenden Wasserfällen. Sie wollen den Bruder von den dunklen Mächten, die ihn entführt haben, zurückverlangen.

Le frère aîné d'un jeune garçon a été enlevé et projeté dans une autre dimension par le Maître des Forces des Ténèbres. Le jeune garçon parvient secrètement à s'introduire dans une vente aux enchères pour délivrer son frère, mais il échoue. Cependant, il est pris en amitié par un géant ressemblant à un léopard qui devient son guide. Ensemble, ils voyagent à travers un monde mystérieux qui ressemble à un rêve, avec ses paysages enchantés et ses chutes d'eau flamboyantes, cherchant sans relâche à arracher son frère aux forces sombres qui se sont emparées de lui.

Hothouse

The artist had read 'Hothouse' by Brian Aldiss years before he became a professional fantasy artist, and loved the atmosphere that prevades the book. So when the opportunity came along to illustrate the book he jumped at the chance. Illustrated here is the moment when two girls, deep in the world-encompassing Banyan forest, encounter a predator attracted by movement. The girls try to stay as still as possible, hoping they can kill it with their humble weapons. The artist imagined their hair with flowers as a result of naturally occurring epiphytic plants growing there rather than being placed in their hair. These would act as aids to both beauty and camouflage.

Años antes de convertirse en ilustrador profesional de fantasía, Tim White había leído "Hothouse" de Brian Aldiss y le había entusiasmado el ambiente que describe el libro. Así que cuando surgió la oportunidad de ilustrar el libro, la recogió al vuelo. Aquí vemos ilustrado el momento en que dos muchachas, que se encuentran en el corazón del infinito bosque Banyan, se topan con un animal depredador atraído por el movimiento. Las muchachas intentan permanecer lo más quietas posible con la esperanza de poder matarlo con sus humildes armas. El ilustrador imaginó sus cabellos engalanados con flores como resultado del crecimiento natural de las plantas epífitas en lugar de la simple colocación artificial de flores en el pelo. Dichas flores proporcionarían no sólo belleza sino también camuflaje.

Der Künstler hatte "Hothouse" von Brian Aldiss Jahre, bevor er professioneller Fantasy-Künstler geworden war, gelesen und mochte die Atmosphäre dieses Buches. Als sich die Gelegenheit bot, es zu illustrieren, nutzte er sie sofort. Hier wird der Augenblick gezeigt, in dem zwei Mädchen tief im weltumspannenden Banyan-Wald auf ein Raubtier treffen, das auf jede Bewegung reagiert. Die Mädchen ver suchen, so bewegungslos wie möglich zu bleiben, und hoffen, es mit ihren bescheidenen Waffen töten zu können. Der Künstler stellte sich ihr Haar mit Blumen geschmückt vor. Es sind aber Epiphyt-Pflanzen, die auf natürliche Weise im Haar der Mädchen wachsen und nicht zum Schmuck hineingesteckt wurden. So dienen sie gleichzeitig der Schönheit und als Tarnung.

Le dessinateur avait lu le roman "Le Monde Vert" de Brian Aldiss (Ed. J'ai Lu), des années avant de devenir illustrateur professionnel. Il avait aimé l'atmosphère qui émanait du livre. Ainsi, lorsque se présenta l'occasion de l'illustrer, il sauta sur l'occasion. La scène représentée ici est celle où deux filles, au plus profond du monde de la forêt de Banyan, rencontrent un prédateur attiré par leurs mouvements. Les filles tentent de rester autant que possible immobiles, espérant que leurs modestes armes suffiront à vaincre la bête. Le dessinateur a imaginé leurs cheveux fleuris comme le résultat d'un fait naturel: les plantes n'ont pas été posées dans les cheveux, elles y poussent. C'est une contribution de la nature tant à la beauté qu'au camouflage.

Leander

The lone warrior and the dragon is a powerful symbol, a metaphor for the struggle of good over evil. In western cultures the dragon was viewed as evil, an icon of the malign forces at work in the world, and associated with demonic power. Eastern cultures, however, viewed the dragon as more in tune with the natural harmonies of the world, and essentially benign. Yet a few were harmful, as in this case where two Samurai warriors are attacked by a dragon. One warrior is incinerated at the first pass of the flying beast, leaving the lone warrior to battle with the monster, seemingly overwhelmed by the immense power and size of his adversary.

El guerrero solitario y el dragón son un símbolo poderoso, una metáfora de la lucha del bien contra el mal. En las culturas occidentales el dragón era considerado como el mal, como un icono de las fuerzas malignas existentes en el mundo y fue asociado al poder del diablo. Las culturas orientales, sin embargo, consideraban al dragón más a tono con la armonía natural del mundo y como algo esencialmente benigno. Aun así existían unos pocos dañinos, como en este caso en que dos guerreros Samurai son atacados por un dragón. Uno de los guerreros queda calcinado con la primera andanada de la bestia voladora dejando al otro solo para luchar contra el monstruo. El guerrero solitario parece abrumado por la inmensa fuerza y el enorme tamaño de su adversario.

Der einsame Krieger und der Drachen sind eine kraftvolle Metapher, ein Symbol für den Kampf zwischen Gut und Böse. In den westlichen Kulturen wurde der Drachen als das Böse, als Sinnbild der schlechten Gewalten in dieser Welt betrachtet und mit dämonischer Kraft in Verbindung gebracht. Östliche Kulturen sehen den Drachen eher als etwas grundsätzlich Gutartiges, das in Einklang mit der natürlichen Harmonie der Welt steht. Einige Drachen waren allerdings gefährlich, wie im Fall der beiden Samurai-Krieger, die von einem solchen angegriffen wurden. Der eine Krieger verbrannte sofort, als die Bestie nur vorbeiflog, und der andere blieb alleine im Kampf gegen das Monster zurück. Auch er wurde dann anscheinend von der ungeheuren Kraft und Größe seines Gegners überwältigt.

Le couple guerrier solitaire / dragon est un symbole puissant, une métaphore du combat entre le bien et le mal. Dans les cultures occidentales, le dragon est assimilé au mal, c'est le représentant des forces maléfiques au travail dans le monde, il est associé au pouvoir démoniaque. Dans les cultures orientales, au contraire, le dragon est vu comme un accord avec les harmonies naturelles du monde, il est essentiellement doux. Certes, quelques-uns sont malfaisants, comme dans cette scène où deux guerriers samouraïs sont attaqués par un dragon. Un samouraï est brûlé au premier passage du monstre volant. L'autre, devenu guerrier solitaire, combat la bête, dominé par la taille et l'immense pouvoir de son adversaire.

Dragon Drone

A self sustaining terror weapon from a long forgotten interstellar war continues its search for victims to destroy, even though both sides of the war annihilated themselves aeons ago. Without the correct command to stop it, the deadly machine will continue to carry out its mission indefinitely. The painting was used for a calendar of dragons by various artists all of whom were given total freedom. No roughs were needed; the rough was for the artist's use only. The mechanical dragon was taken from an earlier work which fitted the project. It was a design that the artist painted onto a friend's stratocaster guitar, the curves of which can be recognised in the painting. The original dragon had flames and smoke coming from its nose which followed the contours of the guitar.

Un arma, procedente de una guerra interestelar ya olvidada, siembra el pánico al continuar su búsqueda de víctimas aun cuando ambos bandos de la guerra quedaron aniquilados hace eones. Si no disponemos del mandato correcto para detenerla, la mortífera máquina continuará cumpliendo su cometido indefinidamente. Esta ilustración fue utilizada para un calendario de dragones de varios ilustradores, los cuales gozaron de plena libertad para llevar a cabo su obra. No fue necesario hacer boceto; el boceto servía únicamente para el ilustrador. El dragón mecánico fue extraído de un trabajo anterior que encajaba en el proyecto. Fue una imagen que el ilustrador pintó en la guitarra stratocaster de un amigo y las curvas de la misma se pueden apreciar en el dibujo. El dragón original despedía fuego y humo por la nariz y estos elementos seguían el contorno de la guitarra.

Eine Terrorwaffe aus einem längst vergessenen interstellaren Krieg, die sich selbständig gemacht hat, sucht weiter nach Opfern, um sie zu zerstören, obwohl beide Kriegsparteien sich schon vor Ewigkeiten selbst ausgelöscht haben. Gibt man ihr nicht einen bestimmten Befehl aufzuhören, wird die Todesmaschine ihre Mission immer weiter ausführen. Das Gemälde wurde für einen Drachen-Kalender von verschiedenen Künstlern, denen man völlige Freiheit gelassen hatte, benutzt. Entwürfe waren nicht erforderlich; diesen Entwurf fertigte der Künstler für sich selbst an. Der mechanische Drachen stammt aus einer früheren Arbeit, die gut zu dem Projekt paßte. Es war ein Bild, das der Künstler auf die Gitarre eines Freundes gemalt hatte, deren Wölbung man in dem Gemälde noch erkennen kann. Dem ursprünglichen Drachen kamen Flammen und Rauch aus der Nase, die sich an die Konturen der Gitarre anschmiegten.

Une terrifiante arme de mort, reste d'une longue guerre interstellaire oubliée, continue sa recherche de victimes à détruire. Pourtant, les deux parties en conflit se sont annihilées mutuellement depuis des éons. Mais sans la commande correcte pour l'arrêter, la machine à tuer continuera sa mission indéfiniment. Cette peinture a servi pour un calendrier ayant pour thème les dragons, dans lequel tous les artistes avaient carte blanche. Fait rare aux Etats-Unis, l'éditeur n'avait demandé aucune esquisse aux dessinateurs. Le dragon mécanique a été emprunté à un travail plus ancien qui correspondait bien à ce nouveau projet. C'était une décoration que l'artiste avait peinte sur la guitare stratocaster d'un ami. Les courbes caractéristiques de la stratocaster se devinent encore dans le dessin. Le dragon original avait des flammes et de la fumée qui sortaient de ses naseaux pour aller épouser les contours de la guitare.

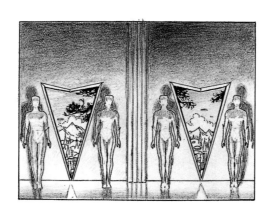

Foundations Friends

On a distant world in its famous golden city some robots have gone berserk, killing many citizens. The large robot population is engaged in a sinister plot to take over the city, but only some of the robots are dangerous. The problem is, there is no way of telling which ones they are. The space federation send a high-ranking security official to oversee the investigations. Yet even here, in rooms in a high security building overlooking the city, one of the servant robots awaits its chance to attack. The smiling faces reveal nothing. Will he have a premonition that something bad is about.to happen, or will he too fall victim to her fatal embrace?

En la famosa ciudad dorada de un mundo lejano hay unos robots que se han vuelto locos y han matado a muchos ciudadanos. La numerosa población robótica se ha enzarzado en el siniestro plan de dominar la ciudad pero sólo algunos de los robots representan un peligro. El problema es que no hay forma de distinguir unos de otros. La Federación Espacial envía a un oficial de seguridad de alta graduación para supervisar la investigación. Pero incluso aquí, en las estancias de un edificio de alta seguridad que domina la ciudad, una de las sirvientas robóticas espera su oportunidad de atacar. Las caras sonrientes no permiten entrever nada. ¿Tendrá el presentimiento de que algo malo está a punto de suceder o caerá víctima del abrazo mortal?

In einer entfernten Welt sind in der berühmten goldenen Stadt ein paar Roboter wild geworden und töten die Stadtbewohner. Die große Roboterbevölkerung ist in ein unheimliches Komplott verwickelt, die Stadt an sich zu reißen, aber nur einige der Roboter sind gefährlich. Das Problem liegt darin, daß man unmöglich wisssen kann, welche von ihnen es sind. Die Raumföderation schickt einen hochrangigen Sicherheitsbeamten, der die Ermittlungen leiten soll. Aber sogar hier, in den Räumen eines Hochsicherheitsbaus, der sich hoch über der Stadt erhebt, wartet einer der Roboter im Dienst auf eine Gelegenheit zum Angriff. Sein lächelndes Gesicht verrät nichts. Wird der Agent eine Vorahnung haben, daß etwas Schlimmes unmittelbar bevorsteht, oder wird er der tödlichen Umarmung erliegen?

Sur un monde lointain, dans la célèbre Cité Dorée, les robots sont devenus fous furieux, tuant de nombreux citoyens. La grande masse des robots est engagée dans un complot sinistre pour prendre la ville, mais certains d'entre eux seulement sont dangereux. Le problème est qu'il est impossible de les reconnaître des autres et de les identifier. La fédération Spatiale a envoyé un officier de sécurité de haut rang pour superviser les recherches.
Même ici, dans les chambres de haute sécurité qui dominent la ville, un des robots attend · l'occasion d'attaquer. Mais le visage souriant ne laisse rien transparaître. A t-il la prémonition que quelque chose de terrible va se produire, ou va-t-il, lui aussi, être victime d'une étreinte fatale ?

A Dark Travelling

A door to a parallel world in another dimension has been opened by an eccentric inventor who, unfortunately, is unable to close it again. Weird and malign entities are beggining to come trought, terrorising his family. In response to this threat he builds a robot guardian to protect them. While he is out his son decides to frighten his sistes by introducing her to this scary new member of the family.

Un excéntrico inventor ha abierto una puerta a un mundo paralelo de otra dimensión y, desafortunadamente, no puede cerrarla. Por ella, empiezan a salir seres extraños y malignos que aterrorizan a su familia. En respuesta a esta amenaza construye un guardián robótico para protegerles. En su ausencia, su hijo decide asustar a su hermana presentándole a este nuevo miembro de la familia tan aterrador.

Ein exzentrischer Erfinder hat die Tür zu einer Neben-Welt in einer anderen Dimension geöffnet und kann sie unglücklicherweise nicht wieder schließen. Unheimliche, bösartige Wesen dringen ein und beginnen, seine Familie zu terrorisieren. Um dieser Bedrohung zu begegnen, baut er einen Roboter-Wächter, der sie beschützen soll. Als er nicht zu Hause ist, beschließt sein Sohn, die Schwester zu erschrecken, indem er sie dem gruseligen, neuen Familienmitglied vorstellt.

Une porte vers un monde parallèle, dans une autre dimension, a été ouverte par un inventeur excentrique. Malheureusement, il est incapable de la refermer. Des entités étranges et maléfiques commencent à surgir et terrorisent sa famille. En réponse à cette menace, il fabrique un gardien-robot pour protéger les siens. Profitant d'un moment où l'inventeur est absent, son fils décide de faire peur à sa sœur en lui présentant cet étrange et nouveau membre de la famille...

A Jungle of Stars

On an arid planet that no longer possesses a breathable atmosphere the populace live in underground cities and protective domes. A secret intelligence officer has escaped an attack made on the capital city by hostile alien forces who are part of an expanding empire. The officer had no time to warn the other authorities, and he and a handful of other operatives made their escape from the covert surveillance centre. They know that capture would be followed by execution. The planet is of strategic importance to the evil invaders, but the officer's escape has been engineered by another, unknown power. Now, the officer's destiny is linked with the ultimate downfall of the powerful invading empire– an evil and malign force in the galaxy.

En un árido planeta cuya atmósfera es irrespirable la población vive en ciudades subterráneas y bajo cúpulas protectoras. Un oficial de la inteligencia secreta ha escapado a un ataque lanzado contra la capital por fuerzas hostiles alienígenas que forman parte de un imperio en expansión. El oficial no dispuso de tiempo para avisar a las otras autoridades y solamente él y un puñado de operativos consiguieron huir del centro secreto de vigilancia. Eran conscientes de que serían ejecutados si les capturaban. El planeta es de importancia estratégica para los malvados invasores pero la huida del oficial ha sido ingeniada por otra fuerza desconocida. Ahora el destino del oficial está ligado a la caída definitiva del poderoso imperio invasor, una fuerza vil y maligna de la galaxia.

Auf einem ausgetrockneten Planeten, in dessen Atmosphäre man nicht mehr atmen kann, lebt die Bevölkerung in unterirdischen Städten und Schutzgewölben. Als feindliche, fremde Kräfte eines expandierenden Reiches die Hauptstadt angreifen, gelingt es einem Mitarbeiter des Geheimdienstes, dem Angriff zu entkommen. Der Agent hatte jedoch keine Zeit, die Behörden zu warnen-er und eine Handvoll anderer Agenten mußten direkt aus dem versteckten Überwachungszentrum fliehen. Sie wissen, daß sie exekutiert werden, falls man sie fängt. Der Planet hat für die bösartigen Invasoren eine strategische Bedeutung, aber die Flucht des Agenten ist von einer anderen unbekannten Macht eingefädelt worden. Das Schicksal des Agenten hängt nun vom endgültigen Untergang des mächtigen Invasoren ab, der in der Galaxie eine böse, unheilvolle Macht darstellt.

Sur une planète aride qui ne possède plus d'atmosphère respirable, la population vit dans une des cités souterraines et sous des dômes de protection. Un officier des services secrets a échappé à une attaque contre la plus grande des villes, attaque menée par des forces étrangères issues d'un empire en extension. L'officier n'a pas le temps de prévenir les autorités fédérales. Avec une poignée d'hommes, il s'échappe du centre secret de surveillance. Ils savent que s'ils sont pris, ils seront exécutés. La planète est d'une importance stratégique pour les diaboliques envahisseurs. Mais l'évasion de l'officier a été manigancée par un autre pouvoir, une force inconnue. Maintenant, le destin de l'officier est lié à l'effondrement de l'empire envahisseur, puissance malfaisante et diabolique qui ronge la galaxie.

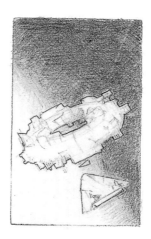

Stars like Dust

On a main route to the stars a lonely way station slowly turns one of a chain of such stations at strategic points throughout the interstellar highway, it is a stopping-off point for starships on their way to the further reaches of the galaxy. These stations provide a rescue service for starships who may have encountered problems during their voyages, or been damaged by unforeseen circumstances such as that caused by passengers can 'board passing starships to take them to far flung destinations.

Una solitaria estación de paso gira lentamente en una ruta principal hacia las estrellas. Es una de las muchas situadas en puntos estratégicos de la autopista interestelar. Son zonas donde se pueden detener las naves estelares que van a los puntos más alejados de la galaxia. Estas estaciones prestan un servicio de rescate a las naves estelares que pueden haber tenido problemas durante sus viajes o que pueden haber resultado dañadas por circunstancias imprevistas, como las causadas por materia interestelar. También son puntos de encuentro para el tráfico del sistema estelar cercano, donde los pasajeros aprovechan para subir a bordo de las naves que pasan por allí para llevarles a destinos lejanos.

Eine einsame Wegstation, die an einer Hauptstraße zu den Sternen liegt, reiht sich in eine Kette von Stationen ein, die an strategischen Punkten auf der interstellaren Autobahn eingerichtet sind. Es sind Haltestellen für Sternenschiffe auf ihrem Weg in ferne Galaxien. Diese Stationen bieten Rettungsdienste für Sternenschiffe, die auf ihrer Reise Probleme bekommen haben oder durch unvorhersehbare Unfälle, z.B. Kollisionen mit interstellaren Körpern, beschädigt worden sind. Es sind auch Knotenpunkte im Verkehr mit benachbarten Sternensystemen; hier können Fahrgäste an Bord von vorbeikommenden Sternenschiffen gehen, die sie zu den entferntesten Reisezielen bringen.

Sur une des grandes routes vers les étoiles, une station solitaire tourne lentement sur elle-même. C'est l'une des nombreuses stations placées aux points stratégiques, le long de l'autoroute interstellaire. C'est une étape pour les vaisseaux dans leur course vers les points les plus lointains de la galaxie. Ces stations sont munies de services de secours pour les vaisseaux qui ont pu rencontrer des problèmes durant leur voyage, être endommagés dans des circonstances imprévues.

Garden at the Edge of Forever

On the most distant inhabited planet of the galaxy a garden sits beneath a star-spangled sky. The garden and its crystal-like building is a lovely place to be, with beautiful views of heaven's vault. The wondrous galaxy dominates the night sky and lights the darkness with its pale light. The light from the far side of the galaxy takes 100.000 years to reach this planet, so the view of the heavens is also a view back in time. Beyond this remote world is the inmensity of intergalactic space. Originally, the rough had a moon, but the art director preferred the artist's idea of a galaxy in the same position.

En el planeta habitado más distante de la galaxia se encuentra un jardín bajo de un cielo salpicado de estrellas. El jardín y su edificio de cristal constituyen un lugar espléndido para estar en él contemplando hermosas vistas de la cúpula celeste. La prodigiosa galaxia domina el cielo nocturno e ilumina la oscuridad con su pálida luz. La luz del lado lejano de la galaxia tarda 100.000 años en llegar a este planeta por lo que la visión de los cielos es también una visión retrospectiva en el tiempo. Más allá de este mundo remoto se encuentra la inmensidad del espacio intergaláctico. De origen, el boceto tenía una luna pero el director artístico prefirió la idea del ilustrador de una galaxia en la misma posición.

Auf dem entferntesten unbewohnten Planeten der Galaxie gibt es einen Garten unter dem sternenübersäten Himmel. Der Garten ist mit seinem kristallenen Gebäude ein herrlicher Ort, dessen Lage unter dem Himmelsgewölbe zauberhaft ist. Die wunderbare Galaxie beherrscht den nächtlichen Himmel und erhellt die Dunkelheit mit ihrem fahlen Licht. Da das Licht 100 000 Jahre braucht, um vom äußersten Ende der Galaxie diesen Planeten zu erreichen, ist der Blick auf den Himmel auch ein Blick zurück in die Zeit. Hinter dieser entfernten Welt liegt der intergalaktische Raum in seiner ganzen Unermeßlichkeit. Auf dem Entwurf gab es ursprünglich einen Mond, aber der Art-Director stimmte dann der Idee des Künstlers zu, an diese Stelle eine Galaxie zu setzen.

Sur la plus lointaine des planètes inhabitées de la galaxie, un jardin attend sous le ciel parsemé d'étoiles. Le jardin et sa construction de cristal forment un endroit où il est agréable de se tenir, la vue sur la voûte céleste y est magnifique. La merveilleuse galaxie domine le ciel nocturne et éclaire les ténèbres de son pâle éclat. La lumière venue des confins de la galaxie met cent mille ans pour atteindre cette planète. La vue du ciel est donc aussi une vue du passé. Au-delà de ce monde écarté, il n'y a plus rien que l'immensité de l'espace intergalactique. A l'origine, une lune figurait sur le croquis préparatoire, mais le directeur artistique a préféré suivre l'idée de l'artiste de la remplacer par une galaxie.

White Moon, Red Dragon

Tired of the city, a princess, having dismissed her entourage, pages her personal shuttlecraft which will shortly arrive in the shuttlebay. In her palace, high above the teeming streets of the mighty Chinese Empire's capital city, she sometimes feels the need to escape the obligations of her duties; to seek peace of mind in some far flung destination. As an accomplished pilot she will fly the semi-automatic craft herself.

Eine Prinzessin, die die Stadt satt und ihr Gefolge weggeschickt hat, läßt ihren persönlichen Flieger ausrufen, der kurz darauf auf dem Landeplatz ankommen wird. In ihrem Palast hoch über den wimmelnden Straßen der Hauptstadt des mächtigen chinesischen Reiches hat sie manchmal das Bedürfnis, all ihren Verpflichtungen zu entfliehen, sich ein möglichst weit entferntes Ziel zu suchen, um dort den inneren Frieden zu finden. Da sie eine vollendete Pilotin ist, wird sie die halbautomatische Maschine selber fliegen.

Cansada de la ciudad, una princesa que ha despedido a su séquito, hace llamar a su nave espacial personal que llegará en breve al puerto espacial. En su palacio, que domina las abarrotadas calles de la poderosa capital del Imperio Chino, ella siente, a veces, la necesidad de escapar a sus deberes y obligaciones con el fin de buscar la paz espiritual en algún punto lejano. Como piloto consumado que es, ella misma pilota la nave semiautomática.

Lassée de la ville, une princesse congédie son entourage et commande sa navette personnelle. Celle-ci arrive rapidement dans le tunnel. Dans son palais, loin au-dessous des rues grouillantes de la capitale du mythique Empire chinois, elle ressent de temps à autre le besoin d'échapper aux obligations de sa charge. Elle cherche alors la paix de l'esprit dans quelque destination lointaine. En pilote accomplie, elle dirige elle-même le véhicule semi-automatique.

One Million Tomorrows

While he is away 'off planet' a star traveller's solar powered house and its elegant grounds are tended by an array of robots. Always seeming to know when he will return from his distant travels his favourite cat lingers by the gateway.

Mientras se encuentra "fuera del planeta", un ejército de robots atiende la casa, provista de energía solar y los jardines ornamentales de un viajero estelar. Aparentemente consciente de cuándo regresará de sus lejanos viajes, su gato favorito permanece junto a la verja de entrada.

Während ein Sternenreisender seinen Planeten verlassen hat, werden sein solarbetriebenes Haus und seine eleganten Anlagen von einem Aufgebot an Robotern gehütet. Seine Lieblingskatze, die immer zu wissen scheint, wann er von seinen Fernreisen zurückkehren wird, sitzt neben dem Tor.

Loin de sa planète d'ancrage, une maison, accompagnée de ses multiples robots, voyage à travers les étoiles, propulsée à l'énergie solaire. Le chat, flânant à la grande porte, semble toujours savoir quand il reviendra de ses lointains voyages.

Sunshaker's War

Two friends accidently find a pathway that leads to another world. Amazed
by their find they go back again and again to explore this apparently uninhabited
world. But uninhabited it is not and strange beings capture one of them. Escaping
to safety the other boy cannot leave his friend and returns in an attempt to save him.
The rough for the painting was given the go-ahead, but the art-director
insisted on the inclusion of the 'Alice in Wonderland' creature of
the sea-lion -half fish, half lion- seen in the foreground.

Dos amigos encuentran, accidentalmente, un camino que lleva a otro mundo.
Asombrados por su hallazgo, van una y otra vez a explorar este mundo
aparentemente deshabitado. Pero no es cierto que esté deshabitado y
unos extraños seres capturan a uno de ellos. El otro muchacho escapa pero
no puede abandonar a su amigo y decide volver en un intento de salvarle.
El boceto recibió la aprobación pero el director artístico insistió en la inclusión
de la criatura del león marino (medio león, medio pez) de
"Alicia en el país de las Maravillas", que se ve en primer plano.

Zwei Freunde finden durch Zufall einen Weg, der in eine andere
Welt führt. Erstaunt über ihre Entdeckung kehren sie immer wieder zurück, um
diese anscheinend unbewohnte Welt zu erforschen. Doch sie ist nicht unbewohnt,
und einer der beiden Freunde wird von merkwürdigen Wesen gefangen.
Der andere Junge, der entkommen konnte, will seinen Freund
nicht allein lassen und geht zurück, um ihn zu retten.
Der Entwurf für das Gemälde wurde prinzipiell akzeptiert,
aber der Art-Director bestand darauf, die "Alice im Wunderland"–Figur des
Meerlöwen-halb Fisch, halb Löwe-, die man im Vordergrund sieht, einzufügen.

Deux amis ont accidentellement trouvé un sentier qui mène à un autre monde.
Emerveillés par leur découverte ils y retournent fréquemment pour explorer
ce monde apparemment inhabité. Pourtant, il n'est pas vraiment désert...
D'étranges êtres capturent l'un des deux garçons. L'autre parvient à s'échapper,
mais il ne peut se résoudre à abandonner son ami. Pour tenter de le délivrer,
il s'aventure de nouveau dans ce monde étrange.
L'esquisse de cette peinture a été immédiatement acceptée par le directeur
artistique , qui a cependant tenu à inclure une créature issue d'"Alice au Pays des
Merveilles": le Lion de Mer, être mi-lion, mi-poisson, que l'on voit au second plan.

Star of Danger

Gliding down a deserted misty street, this misterious denizen of a remote world is shunned by the inhabitants of the town. The creature -thankfully rarely seen- is however, highly dangerous and possesses strange abilities. One of these is the use of a powerful electric field that surrounds it, and which is of such high energy it can kill. Although usually avoiding settlements, they are seen from time to time - much to the disquiet of the local inhabitants.

Mientras se desliza por una neblinosa calle desierta, el misterioso morador de un mundo remoto es rehuido por los habitantes de la ciudad. La criatura, que por fortuna vemos muy rara vez, posee habilidades extremadamente peligrosas. Una de ellas es el empleo de un campo de energía eléctrica que lo envuelve por completo y que es de tal potencia que puede llegar a matar. Aunque suele evitar las poblaciones, de vez en cuando llega a una de ellas, para desasosiego de sus habitantes.

Dieser mysteriöse Bewohner einer abgelegenen Welt, der am Ende einer verlassenen nebligen Straße steht, wird von den Einwohnern der Stadt gemieden. Das Wesen, das sich glücklicherweise nur selten blicken läßt, ist höchst gefährlich und besitzt merkwürdige Fähigkeiten. Es hat zum Beispiel ein starkes elektrisches Feld um sich, dessen enorme Energie tödlich sein kann. Normalerweise meiden diese Wesen jegliche Siedlungen, aber manchmal werden sie doch gesichtet - sehr zur Beunruhigung der Ortsansässigen.

Un mystérieux visiteur venu d'un monde lointain se glisse dans la brume d'une rue déserte. Les habitants de la ville se détournent de son chemin. La créature, qu'heureusement peu de personnes croisent, est de toute façon très dangereuse. Elle possède d'étranges pouvoirs, comme celui de s'entourer d'un puissant champ électrique, d'une intensité si élevée qu'il peut être mortel. Bien que ces étranges visiteurs évitent les endroits trop fréquentés, il arrive qu'ils soient de temps à autre aperçus et c'est déjà trop pour les habitants du lieu.

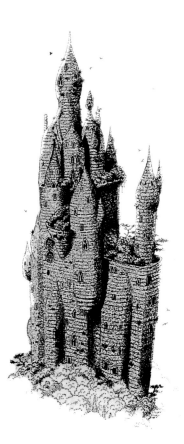

Wheel of Winds

Although its sun wanders in the heavens, the sun never sets on this world.
The other side of the planet is always in darkness, lit only by the myriad stars.
Two separate cultures have envolved who war with each other on the terminator
where the shadows begin. Great fortresses are built to protect the frontier.
This fortress guards a river that runs into the land of shadows.
The rough of the fortress was quite detailed. The landscape was
just in outline and now is lost.

Aun cuando su hijo pasea por los cielos, el sol nunca se pone en este mundo. El otro
lado del planeta está siempre oscuro, iluminado tan solo por las innumerables estrellas.
Han evolucionado dos culturas separadas que pelean entre sí en la frontera donde
empiezan las sombras. Construyen una gran fortaleza para proteger la frontera. Esta
fortaleza está junto a un río que se adentra en la tierra de las sombras.
El boceto de la fortaleza era muy detallado. El paisaje fue ejecutado
a grandes trazos y ahora se ha perdido.

Obwohl die Sonne über den Himmel wandert, scheint die Sonne nur auf einer
Seite des Planeten. Die andere Hälfte liegt immer im Dunkeln und wird nur durch
Myriaden von Sternen erhellt. Zwei verschiedene Kulturen haben sich entwickelt
und bekämpfen sich nun auf dem Terminator, dort, wo der Schatten beginnt. Um
die Grenze zu schützen, werden mächtige Festungen gebaut. Diese Festung
wacht über einen Fluß, der ins Schattenland führt.
Der Entwurf für die Festung war ziemlich detailliert. Die Landschaft
war nur in Umrissen gezeichnet und ist jetzt ganz verschwunden.

Malgré le vagabondage du soleil à travers la voûte céleste, ses rayons n'illuminent
qu'une partie de ce monde. L'autre face de la planète demeure perpétuellement
dans les ténèbres, éclairée seulement par les myriades d'étoiles constellant le ciel noir.
Dans la bande où commence l'ombre, où le jour n'est qu'un crépuscule permanent,
une guerre sans merci oppose les deux cultures. D'immenses forteresses se dressent
pour protéger la frontière. L'une d'entre elles garde une rivière
qui court à travers le pays des ombres.

Blood of Amber

A girl has a rare and magical inherited ability to travel between
possible worlds. This amazing feat is achieved using a combination
of will and an enchanted pack of cards. By thinking about
the destination on each card she is able
to vanish from one place and appear in another, travelling at
the speed of thought. Earth is but one of these worlds.
For this paiting a combination of elements from both
roughs was used for the final image.

Una muchacha posee la extraña y mágica habilidad de viajar
entre mundos posibles. Esta hazaña la consigue combinando su voluntad y
una baraja de naipes encantada. Al concentrarse y otorgar a cada carta un
destino, consigue desaparecer de un lugar y aparecer en otro, viajando a
la velocidad del pensamiento. La Tierra no es más que uno de estos mundos.
Para la imagen final de esta ilustración se utilizó
una combinación de elementos de ambos bocetos.

Ein Mädchen hat die seltene, magische Gabe geerbt, zwischen möglichen
Welten hin und her zu reisen. Diese erstaunliche Leistung gelingt ihr
dank ihrer Willenskraft und einem verzauberten Kartenspiel. Indem sie bei
jeder Karte an den Bestimmungsort denkt, kann sie an einem Ort verschwinden
und an einem anderen wieder auftauchen. Sie bewegt sich dabei mit der
Geschwindigkeit von Gedanken fort. Die Erde ist nur eine dieser möglichen Welten.
In die endgültige Fassung dieses Gemäldes gingen verschiedene
Elemente der beiden Entwürfe ein.

Une jeune fille a hérité d'un pouvoir magique exceptionnel: elle peut voyager
entre les univers, entre tous les mondes possibles. Cet extraordinaire exploit
requiert une très forte volonté et un jeu de cartes enchantées. En se concentrant sur
chaque carte, imaginant une destination, la jeune fille est capable de disparaître
d'un endroit pour apparaître à un autre, voyageant à la vitesse de la pensée.
La terre n'est qu'une de ses multiples destinations.
Le dessinateur a combiné deux esquisses pour réaliser la peinture définitive.

Snows of darkover

A visitor to a remote world with medieval culture experiences a vision which is no dream. She sees three women in black, with dark birds wheeling in the sky behind them. The central figure holds up a mirror in which the woman sees herself, but the image changes to that of a monster. The women are silent and stare at her enigmatically. The image fades and she is left with a feeling of foreboding. Was it a warning? A portent of disaster? The origin rough of the women in black (centre) was changed to make their medieval dress more apparent. The artist used a cut-out of the proof to see how it might look (left), then the final image was painted. The finished proof is seen on the right.

Die Besucherin einer entfernten Welt, deren Kultur dem Mittelalter ähnelt, hat eine Vision, die kein Traum ist. Sie sieht drei Frauen in Schwarz, hinter denen dunkle Vögel am Himmel kreisen. Die zentrale Figur hält einen Spiegel hoch, in dem sie sich selbst sieht, aber ihr Bild verwandelt sich in das eines Monsters. Die anderen Frauen schweigen und starren sie rätselhaft an. Als das Bild verschwimmt, bleibt der Frau ein ungutes Gefühl. War das eine Warnung? Ein böses Omen? Der Künstler wich vom Originalentwurf der Frauen in Schwarz (Mitte) ab, um ihre mittelalterliche Kleidung stärker zu betonen. Dafür benutzte er einen Ausschnitt aus dem Probeabzug, um zu sehen, wie es aussehen würde (links), dann malte er das endgültige Gemälde. Der fertige Druck ist rechts zu sehen.

Una visitante de un mundo remoto con una cultura medieval experimenta una visión que no es un sueño. Ve a tres mujeres vestidas de negro, con oscuros pájaros girando en el cielo detrás de ellas. La figura central sostiene un espejo en el cual la mujer se contempla, pero la imagen cambia a la de un monstruo. Las mujeres permanecen en silencio y la miran fija y enigmáticamente. La imagen se desvanece y ella se queda con un sentimiento premonitorio. ¿Fue un aviso? ¿Una advertencia de tragedia inminente? El boceto original de las mujeres ataviadas de negro (en el centro) fue modificado para hacer que sus ropas medievales fueran más vistosas. El ilustrador utilizó un recorte de la prueba para averiguar cómo se vería (a la izquierda), luego pasó a pintar la imagen definitiva. La prueba final se ve a la derecha.

Une femme visite un monde lointain, un monde de culture médiévale, et fait l'expérience d'une vision qui n'est pas un rêve. De sombres oiseaux tournoient dans le ciel au-dessus de trois femmes vêtues de noir. La silhouette centrale brandit un miroir dans lequel la voyageuse aperçoit son propre reflet, mais l'image se transforme en celle d'un monstre. Les trois femmes sont silencieuses et la regardent d'un air énigmatique. L'image se brouille et la voyageuse reste avec un sombre pressentiment. Etait-ce un avertissement? Le présage d'un terrible évènement? L'esquisse originale de la femme en noir, au centre, a été modifiée pour mieux mettre en évidence son costume médiéval. Avant de passer à la peinture, le dessinateur a utilisé un montage sur épreuve pour voir à quoi pourrait ressembler l'image définitive.

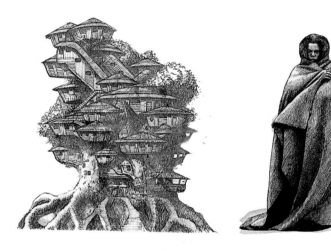

The Fires of Lan Kern

The lone survivor of a nuclear accident aboard a submarine finds himself propelled through time to a strange future world: a world ruled by magic superstitions and dark powers. In the locality where he finds himself an evil witch rules the land from her sinister wooden stronghold.
She sacrifices the local inhabitants for her dark magic.
The survivor, now trapped in this world, feels compelled to stop the evil.
The rough of the house, together with another drawing, was lost by the publishers during the compilation of the artist's first book 'The Science Fiction and Fantasy World of Tim White'.
Only this photostat remains.

Nach einem Atomunfall wird der einzige Überlebende, der sich an Bord eines U-Bootes befindet, in die Zukunft versetzt, in eine merkwürdige Welt, die von Aberglauben und dunklen Kräften beherrscht wird. Er findet sich in einer Gegend wieder, über die eine böse Hexe von einer unheimlichen, hölzernen Festung aus regiert. Sie benutzt die Einwohner als Opfer für ihre dunkle Zauberei. Der Überlebende, der nun in dieser Welt gefangen ist, glaubt, das Böse aufhalten zu müssen.
Den Entwurf für das Haus haben die Verleger zusammen mit einer anderen Zeichnung verloren, als sie das erste Buch des Künstlers "The Science Fiction and Fantasy World of Tim White" zusammenstellten. Es gibt nur noch diese Kopie.

El único superviviente de un accidente nuclear a bordo de un submarino se ve propulsado a través del tiempo hacia un extraño mundo futuro. Es un mundo dominado por las supersticiones mágicas y los poderes oscuros. En la localidad donde él está, una malvada bruja domina el territorio desde su siniestro fortín de madera. Sacrifica a los habitantes del lugar a su magia oscura. El superviviente, que ahora se encuentra atrapado en este mundo, se siente obligado a detener el mal.
Los editores perdieron el boceto de la casa, junto con otro dibujo, durante la compilación del primer libro del ilustrador, "The Science Fiction and Fantasy World of Tim White". Solamente nos queda esta copia fotostática.

Seul survivant d'une catastrophe à bord d'un sous-marin nucléaire, un homme se retrouve projeté à travers le temps vers un étrange monde futur. Un monde soumis aux lois de la magie et aux forces noires. A l'endroit où il échoue, une sorcière maléfique gouverne le pays depuis sa sinistre maison fortifiée. Elle s'empare d'habitants du lieu pour les sacrifier à sa magie noire. L'homme, prisonnier de ce monde, se sent obligé d'agir pour arrêter le mal.
L'esquisse de la maison, ainsi qu'un autre dessin, ont été perdus par l'éditeur lors de la préparation du premier livre de l'artiste: "The Science Fiction and Fantasy World of Tim White". Il n'en reste que ce cliché.

A Wizard Abroad

A portal in a tumulus, or burial mound, shows a glimpse of an enchanted world beyond - the land of the mysterious people of the faity barrows. This is the world of the 'Sidhe' - elemental beings of irish folklore - who can, at certain times, enter our reality. Humans entering through the portal, however, may find the gateway closing behind them and vanishing, leaving no means of escape and trapping them there forever. The knot-work border is typical of the kind of works found on stone monuments throughout Ireland and the British Isles. The ancient Celtic peoples had a deep belief in these magical other worlds and their strange and secretive inhabitants.

Un pórtico en un túmulo o montículo funerario nos permite vislumbrar el mundo encantado que existe más allá: la tierra del misterioso pueblo de los montículos de las hadas. Éste es el mundo de los "Sidhe", seres elementales del folklore irlandés que, en ciertos momentos, pueden entrar en nuestra realidad. Sin embargo, los humanos que cruzan el portal se arriesgan a que se cierre la puerta tras de ellos y desaparezcan sin vía de escape y atrapados para siempre. El trabajo nudoso del borde es típico e igual al encontrado en monumentos de piedra esparcidos por toda Irlanda y por las islas británicas. Los antiguos pueblos celtas creían profundamente en estos otros mundos mágicos y en sus extraños y secretos habitantes.

Ein Tor in einem Tumulus oder Grabhügel gibt den Blick auf eine Zauberwelt frei - das Land der geheimnisvollen Bewohner der Feenhügel. Es ist die Welt der "Sidhe" Figuren der irischen Volkskunde, die in unsere Wirklichkeit eindringen können. Menschen, die durch das Tor gehen, müssen manchmal feststellen, daß es sich hinter ihnen schließt und verschwindet. Es gibt kein Zurück, sie sind für immer gefangen. Das Motiv des geknoteten Randes findet man an Steinmonumenten in Irland und auf den britischen Inseln. Die alten, keltischen Völker hatten einen tiefen Glauben an diese Zauberwelten und ihre seltsamen, geheimnisvollen Bewohner.

Un portail enfoui dans un antique tertre laisse passer la vision fugitive d'un pays enchanté. C'est le monde des mystérieux habitants du Tumulus, le monde du petit peuple, des fées et des hafelins, ces êtres du folklore irlandais. Leur demeure est le Sidhe, palais souterrain dont l'entrée se trouve dans le Tumulus. Parfois, lorsque ses habitants le désirent, le sidhe peut passer dans notre réalité et être aperçu par les hommes. Mais les imprudents qui franchissent le portail entendent la porte se fermer derrière eux et ils disparaissent à jamais du monde des hommes. Les ornements sont typiques du style de gravure que l'on retrouve sur les pierres des monuments et les menhirs, nombreux à travers l'Irlande et les Iles Britanniques. Les Celtes croyaient profondément en l'existence du monde magique des fées, et tout détail étrange dans la vie quotidienne était imputé au caractère malicieux du petit peuple.

Prince of Chaos

During a long journey, a prince stops at a vast, and seemingly deserted, castle. Using the oportunity to escape from the bitterly cold night outside he ventures in. finding a suitable chamber he builds a fire and makes himself comfortable. Later, almost at the point of sleep in the flickering glow of the firelit room, he notices a cold blue light in a dark stairway gaining in intensity. The prince jumps to his feet. The blue light resolves itself into the apparition of a beautiful woman gliding silently down the spiral staircase. Instinctively drawing his sword the prince, well used to ways of battle, is awed by this spectral woman. But if this is a supernatural threat will his sword protect him from the unearthly visitor?
The pose of the ghost was based on the figure from an earlier jewellery piece made by the artist (see above right).

Durante un largo viaje, un príncipe se detiene en un enorme castillo que parece abandonado. Se aventura a entrar para escapar del frío glacial de la noche. Encuentra una habitación de suagrado, hace una hoguera y acomoda. Más tarde, cuando está casi a punto de dormirse, al tembloroso resplandor del fuego, advierte una fría luz azul, en una oscura escalera, que va ganando intensidad. El príncipe se pone en pie de un salto. La luz azul se transforma en una hermosa mujer que se desliza por la escalera de caracol. El príncipe, avezado en las artes del combate, desenfunda su espada instintivamente al quedar boquiabierto ante la imagen espectral de la mujer. Pero si se trata de una amenaza sobrenatural, ¿le podrá proteger su espada de la visitante?
La pose del fantasma se inspiró en la figura de una joya que había realizado el ilustrador con anterioridad (ver arriba a la derecha).

Auf einer langen Reise hält ein Prinz an einem riesigen, anscheinend verlassenen Schloß an. Er will die Gelegenheit nutzen, der bitterlich kalten Nacht zu entfliehen und wagt sich hinein. Als er ein geeignetes Zimmer gefunden hat, zündet er ein Feuer an und macht es sich bequem. Später, als er im flackernden Licht des vom Feuer erhellten Raumes gerade einschlafen will, bemerkt er plötzlich ein kaltes, blaues Licht auf einer Treppe, das immer stärker wird. Der Prinz springt auf. Das blaue Licht verwandelt sich in die Erscheinung einer schönen Frau, die schweigend die Wendeltreppe hinunterschwebt. Der kampferprobte Prinz, der schon sein Schwert zieht, ist von dieser gespenstischen Frau vor Ehrfurcht wie erstarrt. Aber wenn dies eine übernatürliche Bedrohung ist, wird sein Schwert ihn vor der überirdischen Besucherin schützen?
Die Haltung des Geistes geht auf die Figur eines Schmuckstückes zurück, das der Künstler angefertigt hat (siehe oben rechts).

A l'issue d'une longue et harassante journée de voyage, un prince fait halte dans un immense château. Celui-ci semble désert. Le soleil décline et le prince ne tient pas à affronter la nuit froide et piquante. Il se risque donc à chercher une chambre convenable, y allume un feu et s'installe confortablement. Plus tard dans la nuit, à l'instant où le prince allait s'endormir, il remarque en direction de l'escalier une petite lumière bleue qui perce le rougeoiement vacillant de la pièce éclairée par le feu. Le prince, immédiatement réveillé, saute sur ses pieds. La lumière bleue gagne en intensité et se transforme en une très belle femme. Elle regarde silencieusement vers le bas de l'escalier en spirale. Le prince, aguerri par de multiples combats, tire instinctivement son épée, mais il est saisi d'une crainte respectueuse devant l'apparition spectrale. S'il s'agit d'une menace surnaturelle, son épée le protégera elle de ce visiteur venu d'un autre monde?
La posture du fantôme est inspirée d'un bijou réalisé avant par l'artiste lui-même.

Bluebells

In classical mythology nearly every natural thing - like streets, rivers, lakes, mountains, and springs - had its own divinity, personified in the form of a female nymph, young and beautiful. These spirits were usually benevolent towards mortals. Here, nymphs of flowers revel in just being alive.

In der klassischen Mythologie besaß beinahe jede Naturerscheinung-Bäume, Flüße, Seen, Gebirge und Quellen-ihre eigene Gottheit, die in der Gestalt von jungen, schönen Nymphen verkörpert wurde. Diese Geister waren den Sterblichen in der Regel zugetan. Hier haben Blumennymphen ihre Freude daran, einfach nur zu leben.

En la mitología clásica casi todos los elementos de la naturaleza (árboles, ríos, lagos, montañas y manantiales) poseían su propia divinidad personificada en la forma de una ninfa, joven y hermosa. Estos espíritus solían ser benévolos para con los mortales. Aquí, las ninfas de las flores se deleitan con el simple hecho de estar vivas.

Dans la mythologie classique, chacun des éléments naturels, comme les chemins, les rivières, les lacs, les montagnes, les sources, avait sa propre divinité personnifiée sous la forme d'une jeune et jolie nymphe. Ces esprits étaient généralement bienveillants envers les mortels. Ici, les nymphes des fleurs se divertissent et se réjouissent tout simplement d'exister.

Eye of the Cat

Discovering through his magic that an evil extra-terrestrial entity is coming to earth to kill many people, a Navajo Shaman decides he cannot idly sit by and allow this to happen. Using his skill in the ancient art of sand-paiting he creates a magic portal through which he will travel in order to stop this evil— if he can.

Al descubrir, por medio de sus poderes mágicos, que un vil ente extraterrestre viene a la tierra para matar gente, un chamán navajo decide intentar evitarlo. Utilizando sus habilidades en el antiguo arte de la pintura de arena crea un portal mágico a través del cual viajará para detener el mal... si es que puede.

Ein Navajo-Schamane, der durch seine Zauberkunst entdeckt hat, daß ein böses außerirdisches Wesen auf die Erde kommen wird, um dort etliche Menschen zu töten, beschließt, daß er nicht untätig zusehen kann, wie es dazu kommt. Mit Hilfe der uralten Kunst des Sandzeichnens bildet er ein Zaubertor, durch das er reisen will, um das Böse aufzuhalten-wenn es ihm gelingt.

Par le truchement de sa magie, un sorcier navajo découvre qu'une entité extraterrestre maléfique est en route pour la terre et va exterminer des populations entières. Le sorcier refuse de laisser s'accomplir une telle monstruosité et décide d'intervenir. Grâce à son adresse dans l'art ancien des signes sur le sable, il crée une porte magique à travers laquelle il pourra voyager pour aller à la rencontre du mal et tenter de l'arrêter.

Frost and Fire

The strange relationship of two warring lovers comes to an apparently tragic end. The two planetary explorers find a fantastic treasure, but the girl is injured. Given the choice of his lover or the treasure, her heartless companion chooses the latter, leaving her to die on this frozen world. But a strange, planet-encompassing plant lies hidden beneath the permaflost, and it absorbs the girl and her mind. The plant controls both the world and its weather. Years later the planet becomes a resort, its harsh, icy weather held in check by a super-computer. The girl's lover returns to the planet and is drawn to the place where he left her. He also meets a tragic end, and his mind is absorbed by the computer. Thus the two lovers - now invisible, disembodied, and immortal - continue their stormy relationship on a planetary scale.

La extraña relación entre dos amantes que se hacen la guerra llega a un final aparentemente trágico. Los dos exploradores planetarios encuentran un fantástico tesoro pero la chica resulta herida. Cuando su desalmado compañero ha de elegir entre el tesoro o ella, elige el primero abandonándola para que muera en este mundo glacial. Pero una extraña planta que habita en todo el planeta yace oculta debajo del permafrost y absorbe tanto a la chica como a su mente. La planta controla el mundo y el clima. Años después el planeta se convierte en un lugar vacacional donde el duro clima es controlado por una macrocomputadora. El amante de la muchacha regresa al planeta y se siente atraído hacia el lugar donde la abandonó. Él también encuentra un trágico final y su mente es absorbida por el ordenador. De este modo los dos amantes, ahora invisibles, incorpóreos e inmortales, continúan su tormentosa relación a escala planetaria.

Die merkwürdige Beziehung eines gegensätzlichen Liebespaares findet ein scheinbar tragisches Ende. Die beiden planetaren Forscher finden einen fantastischen Schatz, aber das Mädchen ist verletzt. Vor die Wahl zwischen seiner Geliebten oder dem Schatz gestellt, entscheidet sich der herzlose Freund für letzteren und läßt seine Freundin zurück, auf daß sie in dieser eisigen Welt sterbe. Aber versteckt unter dem Dauerfrost liegt eine seltsame Pflanze, die den ganzen Planeten umspannt. Sie absorbiert das Mädchen und seinen Geist. Die Pflanze kontrolliert die Welt und ihr Wetter. Jahre später wird der Planet zu einem Erholungsort, denn sein rauhes, eisiges Wetter wird von einem Super-Computer kontrolliert.
Der Freund des Mädchens kehrt auf den Planeten zurück, und es zieht ihn an den Ort hin, wo er sie verlassen hat. Auch er findet nun ein tragisches Ende: sein Geist wird von dem Computer absorbiert. So führt das Paar, das jetzt unsichtbar, körperlos und unsterblich geworden ist, seine stürmische Beziehung von nun an auf planetarischer Ebene fort.

Les étranges relations entre deux amants qui se déchirent semblent se précipiter vers une fin tragique. Ils exploraient une planète gelée lorsqu'ils ont trouvé un fantastique trésor. Mais la fille fut blessée et son état a contraint son compagnon à choisir entre elle et le trésor. L'homme sans cœur a choisi le trésor, laissant sa compagne sur ce monde glacé.
Une plante étrange, organisme unique et pourtant présent partout sur ce monde, enfouie sous le sol gelé, enserrant le sol de la planète entière dans ses racines, a absorbé le corps et l'esprit de la fille. Cette plante contrôle à la fois la planète et son climat. Des années plus tard, la planète est colonisée grâce à un super ordinateur qui permet une régulation du climat. L'amant de la fille revient sur la planète et se sent attiré vers l'endroit où il l'a abandonnée. Mais, arrivé sur place, il rencontre une fin tragique, et son esprit est absorbé par l'ordinateur.

Fire Pattern

S.H.C. or Spontaneous Human Combustion is a strange paranormal event. The victim is almost totally consumed by fire, but other objects nearby remain almost untouched. The heat from this intense fire is enough to render flesh and bone to powdery ash, yet even temperatures of 3000 °F are not enough to destroy bones totally. Consequently the unnatural fire of S.H.C., which often leaves a lingering, blush, sweet-smelling smoke must be especially powerful. A rare phenomenon, little research has been done as victims are few, thus it remains a mystery.

La S.H.C.(combustión humana espontánea) es un extraño suceso paranormal. La víctima es consumida por el fuego casi por completo pero otros objetos próximos permanecen casi intactos. El calor desprendido de este fuego intenso es suficiente para convertir carne y huesos en cenizas, aunque las temperaturas que alcanzan los 1600°C no son suficientes para destruir totalmente los huesos. En consecuencia el fuego artificial de la combustión humana espontánea, que a menudo deja un humo duradero, azulado y dulzón, debe ser especialmente poderoso. Es un extraño fenómeno poco investigado puesto que las víctimas son pocas y, por tanto, sigue siendo un misterio.

S.H.C. oder Spontaneous Human Combustion (Menschliche Selbstentzündung) ist ein merkwürdiges paranormales Ereignis. Das Opfer wird fast vollständig vom Feuer vernichtet, während andere Gegenstände in der Nähe nahezu unversehrt bleiben. Die Hitze dieses intensiven Feuers ist so stark, daß sie Fleisch und Knochen in pulvrige Asche verwandelt-selbst Temperaturen von 3000 °F reichen nicht aus, um Knochen vollständig zu zerstören. Das unnatürliche Feuer der S.H.C., das oft einen hartnäckigen, bläulichen, süßlich riechenden Rauch zurückläßt, muß dementsprechend besonders stark sein. Ein seltenes Phänomen, das noch nicht gut erforscht ist, da es zu wenig Opfer gibt; es bleibt ein Rätsel.

La C.H.S. ou Combustion Humaine Spontanée est un phénomène paranormal plusieurs fois observé. Il ne s'agit plus d'imaginaire fantastique, mais de véritables énigmes posées à la science. Les victimes sont, en quelques secondes, entièrement consumées par des flammes surgies du corps lui-même, mais les objets environnants sont le plus souvent à peine noircis. La chaleur de cet incroyable brasier est telle que la chair et les os sont transformés en cendres poudreuses, alors que l'on sait que la combustion des os nécessite des températures supérieures à 1600°C. Le pouvoir de ce phénomène est donc extrêmement puissant, et d'autant plus étrange qu'il épargne parfois les vêtements mêmes de la victime. Bien que des cas soient régulièrement signalés et observés, les rapports policiers et médicaux n'ont jamais abouti et ce fait que nul ne peut nier, la combustion spontanée, demeure un mystère.

Nightwish

With some powerful spells a young witch is able to change herself into mist and, merging with the smoke from a magic candle, wanders almost invisibly through the night, going where she wills herself. In this state she can enter buildings through keyholes or cracks around windows and doors. There is virtually no building that she cannot eventualy gain access to.

Con unos cuantos conjuros una joven bruja es capaz de convertirse en niebla y, fundiéndose con el humo de una vela mágica, puede pasear de forma casi invisible a través de la noche yendo allí donde quiera. De este modo puede penetrar en edificios a través del ojo de las cerraduras o de las rendijas en puertas y ventanas. Prácticamente no existe edificio al cual no pueda acceder.

Eine junge Hexe kann sich mit Hilfe einiger Zaubersprüche in Nebel verwandeln; indem sie sich mit dem Rauch einer Zauberkerze verbindet, bewegt sie sich beinahe unsichtbar durch die Nacht, wo immer sie hin will. In diesem Zustand kann sie durch Schlüssellöcher oder Ritzen an Fenstern und Türen in Gebäude hineinschlüpfen. Es gibt im Grunde kein Haus, in das sie nicht hineinkommen könnte.

Avec quelques incantations puissantes, une jeune sorcière parvient à se changer en brume et, se mélant à la fumée d'une bougie magique, presque invisible, elle erre à travers la nuit et pénètre partout où elle le désire. Sous cette forme, elle peut s'introduire dans les maisons par le trou de la serrure, ou par les fentes autour des fenêtres et des portes. De fait, aucun bâtiment ne lui est inaccessible.

The Jesus Incident

On a distant world human interstellar travelling colonists have an outpost. The hostile life forms on this planet are so dangerous that the colonists can only survive by living in a virtual fortress. Unbeknown to their superiors, some members of the colony indulge in a foolhardy and hazardous game: they dare each-other to 'run the perimeter' naked for money. Outside the protective walls they are at the mercy of the deadly alien life, and many don't get back. The image uses a symbolic approach to represent both the title and the story. The girl forms the shape of an inverted crucifix, while the demonic creatures who devour those who lose in the perilous game attack her.

En un mundo lejano los colonos humanos que efectúan viajes interestelares tienen un puesto de avanzada. Las hostiles formas de vida de este planeta son tan peligrosas que los colonos sólo pueden sobrevivir viviendo en una auténtica fortaleza. A escondidas de sus superiores, algunos miembrosde la colonia se entregan a un juego peligroso y temerario: se retan unos a otros a echar, desnudos, "la carrera alrededor del perímetro" a cambio de dinero. Fuera de los muros de protección se encuentran a merced de la mortífera forma de vida alienígena y muchos no regresan. La imagen emplea un enfoque simbólico para representar tanto el título como la historia. La muchacha adopta la forma de un crucifijo invertido mientras que las criaturas, que devoran a aquellos que pierden en el arriesgado juego, la atacan.

In einer weit entfernten Welt haben interstellare menschliche Siedler einen Vorposten aufgebaut. Die feindlichen Lebensbedingungen auf diesem Planeten sind so gefährlich, daß die Siedler nur überleben können, weil sie in einer Art Festung leben. Ohne das Wissen ihrer Vorgesetzten frönen einige Mitglieder der Kolonie einem tollkühnen, gefährlichen Spiel: sie fordern sich gegenseitig heraus, für Geld nackt "um das Gelände herumzulaufen". Doch jenseits des Schutzwalls sind sie auf Gedeih und Verderb dem tödlichen außerirdischen Leben ausgeliefert, und viele von ihnen kommen niemals zurück. Das Bild stellt Titel und Geschichte mit symbolischen Mitteln dar. Das Mädchen hat die Form eines umgedrehten Kruzifix und wird von dämonischen Gestalten, die die Verlierer des gefährlichen Spiels verschlingen, angegriffen.

Les colonies de voyageurs interstellaires possèdent un avant-poste sur un monde lointain. Les formes de vie indigènes sont sur cette planète si hostiles et dangereuses que, pour survivre, les colons sont contraints de se barricader dans des forteresses. A l'insu de leurs supérieurs, certains membres de la colonie se laissent aller à un jeu hasardeux et téméraire: ils se défient mutuellement de courir nus à l'extérieur, le long du périmètre de sécurité et prennent des paris dont les enjeux peuvent atteindre des sommes importantes. En dehors des murs protecteurs, ils sont à la merci des cruelles créatures indigènes, et beaucoup ne reviennent pas. L'image utilise une approche symbolique pour représenter à la fois le titre et l'histoire. Les filles forment la silhouette d'un crucifix inversé alors que se produit l'attaque des créatures démoniaquesqui dévorent les perdants de ce jeu dangereux.

Fiends

A demoness lies almost helpless - trapped by a magic vine around her neck. But, possessed of telepathic ability, she can put thoughts of such power into the minds of people within range that they lose touch with their own minds and do whatever she wants. Once the vine is removed the 'telepathic victim' is skinned alive with supernatural strength by the demoness who uses skins to line her nest.
The original rough had the demoness on a bed of human skins as in the narrative. Although this was an accurate rendering from the book, on the grounds of acceptability the publishers decided to avoid the somewhat sinister backdrop and asked for a more innocuous background that would be less controversial.

Una diablesa yace atrapada por una enredadera mágica alrededor del cuello. Pero, al estar dotada de poderes telepáticos, es capaz de introducir pensamientos en la mente de otras personas cercanas con tanta fuerza que éstas pueden llegar a perder el contacto con su propia mente y hacer lo que ella desee. Una vez retirada la enredadera la "víctima telepática" es despellejada viva con la fuerza sobrenatural de la diablesa que utiliza tales pieles para hacerse su nido.
El boceto original mostraba a la diablesa sobre un lecho de pieles humanas. Aunque esta imagen era fiel al libro, los editores se guiaron por los baremos de la aceptación del público y decidieron evitar el siniestro fondo pidiendo un segundo plano más inocuo y menos controvertido.

Eine Dämonin ist von einer magischen Weinrebe um ihren Hals gefangen und liegt hilflos da. Aber da sie telepathische Kräfte besitzt, kann sie die Gedanken aller Menschen in Reichweite so beeinflussen, daß sie ihr eigenes Denken vergessen und tun, was sie will. Sobald die Weinrebe entfernt ist, häutet die Dämonin das "telepathische Opfer" mit Hilfe ihrer übernatürlichen Kraft am lebendigen Leib. Solche Häute benutzt sie, um ihr Nest auszulegen. Im Originalentwurf lag die Dämonin auf einem Bett aus menschlichen Häuten wie in der Erzählung. Obgleich dies eine genaue Wiedergabe des Buches war, entschied der Verleger, dieses recht finstere Dekor zu vermeiden und bat um einen harmloseren, weniger umstrittenen Hintergrund.

Une femme-démon gît sans aide, le cou enserré dans les sarments d'une vigne magique. Mais, possédant un pouvoir télépathique, elle peut produire des pensées d'un formidable pouvoir dans l'esprit des gens, sans que ceux-ci ne s'en aperçoivent, et elle peut ainsi les conduire à agir comme elle le désire. Une fois la vigne arrachée, la victime de la télépathie est écorchée vive par la force surnaturelle du démon femelle, qui en utilisera la peau pour tapisser son repaire.
Bien que ce soit une fidèle référence au livre, l'éditeur a préféré éviter ce renvoi trop sinistre et a demandé un décor plus neutre et moins sujet à polémique.

New Tales of Cthulhu Mythos

A couple accidentally discover a malevolent, evil entity from a sinister realm, existing in our reality. Believing they were unobserved by the horrible thing they plan to do something about it, but who would believe them? Unfortunately for them the entity sensed their presence, and it sends a monstruous, hideous creature with a venomous, fatal bite to destroy them. Having gained access to their dwelling the vile creature downs the girl's companion with its supernatural venom, and is temporarily surprised when the girl enters the room. But she freezes in terror as it turns and lurches towards her, to lash out with another deadly bite.

Una pareja descubre accidentalmente a un ente vil y malévolo procedente de un siniestro reino que existe en nuestra realidad. Al creer que no son observados por esa horrible cosa planean hacer algo pero, ¿quién iba a creerles? Desafortunadamente para ellos, el ente siente su presencia y envía en su contra a una monstruosa y repugnante criatura, cuya mordedura venenosa es letal. Tras haber conseguido acceder a su morada, la vil criatura abate al compañero de la muchacha con su veneno sobrenatural y queda temporalmente sorprendida cuando la muchacha entra en la estancia. Sin embargo, ella queda paralizada por el terror cuando la criatura se gira y se abalanza contra ella para propinarle otra mordedura mortal.

Ein Paar entdeckt zufällig, daß ein böswilliges, übelwollendes Wesen aus einem unheimlichen Reich in unserer Wirklichkeit existiert. In der Annahme, daß das schreckliche Wesen sie nicht beobachtet hat, beschließen sie, etwas dagegen zu tun - doch wer wird ihnen Glauben schenken? Zu ihrem Unglück hat das Wesen sie doch entdeckt, und es schickt ein riesiges, scheußliches Geschöpf los, um sie mit einem giftigen, tödlichen Biß zu zerstören. Als das abscheuliche Geschöpf sich Zugang zu ihrer Wohnung verschafft hat, streckt es den Freund des Mädchen mit seinem übernatürlichen Gift nieder und ist für einen Augenblick überrascht, als das Mädchen den Raum betritt. Doch sie erstarrt vor Schreck, als es sich umdreht und auf sie zu taumelt, um zu einem weiteren tödlichen Biß auszuholen.

Un couple découvre accidentellement une entité malveillante, diabolique, venue d'un royaume sinistre hanter notre réalité. Ne pensant pas qu'ils puissent être observés par l'horrible chose, ils discutent des moyens de l'annihiler. Mais qui voudrait les aider, les croire? Malheureusement pour eux, l'entité a senti leur présence et envoie pour les tuer une créature hideuse, monstrueuse, munie de crocs empoisonnés. Ayant trouvé leur domicile, la terrible créature assassine le compagnon de la fille de son venin surnaturel et reste un instant surprise lorsque cette dernière entre dans la pièce. Mais la fille est saisie d'une terreur glacée lorsque la chose se tourne et se dirige vers elle pour décocher une autre morsure mortelle.

The Stress of her Regard

A couple spend their wedding night at an old inn, but an evil female shape-shifting spirit has fallen in love with the husband. She casts him into an enchanted sleep, and in a frenzied jealous rage she tears apart the body of his wife and then vanishes, leaving him the apparent perpetrator of this grisly murder. Narrowly he escapes a lynch mob, but will he escape his supernatural admirer? By a strange and peculiar coincidence this portion of the book, written by an American author, is set in a locality very near 'The Long Man of Wilmington' (a famous ancient turf cut figure), the artist's mother runs and old inn from which this room is painted. Stranger still, from the window of this room the hill where the Long Man has stood for centuries can be seen, just two miles away!

Una pareja pasa la noche de bodas en una vieja posada pero un espíritu maligno, que adopta la forma femenina, se ha enamorado del marido. El espíritu le sume en un sueño encantado y, presa de un furioso ataque de celos, descuartiza el cuerpo de la esposa para luego esfumarse, dejándole a él como el supuesto autor del repugnante crimen. Él escapa por muy poco a un linchamiento popular pero, ¿podrá escaparse de su admiradora sobrenatural? Por una extraña y curiosa casualidad esta parte del libro, escrita por un autor americano, transcurre en una localidad muy cercana al "Hombre alto de Wilmington" (una famosa y antigua figura realizada en césped), donde la madre del ilustrador regenta una antigua posada desde la cualestá pintada esta habitación. Y, aunque parezca más extraño todavía, desde la ventana de esta habitación se ve, a tan solo dos millas dedistancia, la colina donde se encuentra desde hace siglos el "Hombre alto".

Ein Paar verbringt die Hochzeitsnacht in einem alten Gasthaus, doch ein böser weiblicher Geist, der in verschiedene Gestalten schlüpfen kann, hat sich in den Ehemann verliebt. Sie zaubert ihn in den Schlaf, zerfetzt in rasender Eifersucht den Körper seiner Frau, verschwindet und läßt ihn, den man nun für den Täter dieses gräßlichen Verbrechens hält, zurück. Er entkommt mit knapper Not einem wütenden Mob, der ihn lynchen will-aber wird er auch seiner übernatürlichen Verehrerin entkommen? Durch einen sonderbaren Zufall spielt dieser Teil des Buches, verfaßt von einem amerikanischen Autor, in einer Gegend ganz in der Nähe des "Großen Mannes von Wilmington" (einer berühmten alten Torffigur), wo die Mutter des Künstlers ein altes Gasthaus führt, dessen Zimmer dem Künstler hier als Vorlage dienten. Noch merkwürdiger ist, daß man vom Fenster dieses Zimmers aus in nur zwei Meilen Entfernung den Hügel sehen kann, auf dem seit Jahrhunderten der "Große Mann" steht!

Un couple passe sa nuit de noces dans une vieille auberge, mais un esprit maléfique femelle, capable de changer de forme, tombe amoureux du mari. Elle le plonge dans un sommeil enchanté puis, dans un accès de jalousie rageuse, elle déchire atrocement le corps de la femme avant de disparaître. L'homme reste seul avec le cadavre mutilé, apparemment coupable de l'effroyable meurtre. Il échappe de peu à un lynchage, mais parviendra-t-il à se défaire de sa surnaturelle admiratrice? Par une étrange coïncidence, cette partie du livre, écrite par un auteur américain se passe dans une petite ville du Sussex , en Angleterre, près de laquelle se trouve un intéressant vestige préhistorique, le "Grand Homme de Wilmington". C'est un dessin immense gravé sur le sol, et la végétation est visible de loin. Or, la chambre représentée par l'artiste a été inspirée par l'une des chambres d'une vieille auberge tenue par sa mère, chambre par la fenêtre de laquelle on peut voir le Grand Homme, gravé à flanc de montagne, deux miles plus loin. L'écrivain américain a t-il séjourné chez la mère de l'artiste ?

Trail of Cthulhu

In its lair on a shunned and remote south pacific island, and protected by disciples, an ancient evil god in a slimy dark well is fed by acolytes. They throw kidnapped victims to their dreadful deaths in the jaws of the hideous monster. Its evil influence spreads beyond the island as its sinister power increases.

In ihrer Höhle auf einer gemiedenen, abgelegenen Insel im Südpazifik wird eine alte böse Gottheit von ihren Jüngern beschützt und in einem glitschigen, dunklen Loch sitzend von ihren Gefolgsleuten gefüttert. Sie werfen entführte Opfer hinein, die im Schlund des scheußlichen Monsters einen furchtbaren Tod finden. Sein böser Einfluß reicht schon über die Insel hinaus, denn seine unheimliche Macht wächst immer mehr.

En su guarida de una isla remota y olvidada del sur del Pacífico, protegida por discípulos, un anciano dios del mal es alimentado, en su viscoso pozo, por sus acólitos. Lanzan a las víctimas secuestradas a una muerte espantosa en las fauces del repugnante monstruo. Su maligna influencia se extiende más allá de la isla mientras aumenta su siniestro poder.

Dans une petite île du Pacifique Sud, éloignée à l'écart des routes maritimes, se trouve le repère, protégé par des disciples d'un ancien dieu maléfique. Tapi dans des ténèbres gluantes, il attend d'être nourri par ses serviteurs. Ceux-ci enlèvent des victimes pour les conduire à une mort atroce entre les mâchoires du monstre hideux. Son influence maléfique s'étend au-delà de l'île, au fur et à mesure que s'accroît son sinistre pouvoir.

Dagon

In a noisome and foul-smelling cavern in the depths of hell a hideous demon gorges itself, greedily devouring helpless mortals who have unjustly taken lives in this world. The demon, with others of its order, are well supplied with victims from our earthly dimension.

En una sobrecogedora y pestilente caverna de las profundidades del infierno un repugnante diablo engulle con voracidad a los indefensos mortales que se han visto injustamente privados de la vida en este mundo. El diablo, junto a otros de su misma especie, está bien abastecido de víctimas de nuestra dimensión terrenal.

In einer überriechenden Grotte in den Tiefen der Hölle frißt sich ein abscheulicher Dämon voll; gierig verschlingt er hilflose Sterbliche, die auf der Welt zu Unrecht getötet haben. Der Dämon und andere seiner Art sind mit Opfern aus unseren Erden-Dimensionen gut versorgt.

Dans une caverne fétide et puante des profondeurs de l'enfer, un démon hideux fait un odieux festin, dévorant avidement les malheureux mortels qui ont injustement volé des vies dans notre monde. Compte tenu du grand nombre de criminels dans notre dimension terrestre, ce démon, et plusieurs de ses amis, sont largement approvisionnés.

The Lurking Fear

Thousands of people vanish every year. Obviously some are the victims of accidents or murder, while some intentionally disappear to avoid circumstances. Here, a demon from hell enters our dimension, attracted by the aura of evil people. He comes to collect them, tearing off the victim's heads so they cannot feign death. Their mortal remains vanish, and the demon returns to hell with their souls for the commencement of their eternal tortures.

Jedes Jahr verschwinden Tausende von Menschen. Manche fallen Unfällen oder Morden zum Opfer, aber einige verschwinden auch absichtlich, um Umstände zu vermeiden. Hier dringt ein Dämon aus der Hölle in unsere Dimension ein, angezogen von der Ausstrahlung böser Menschen. Er kommt, um sie einzusammeln und reißt seinen Opfern die Köpfe ab, damit sie sich nicht tot stellen können. Ihre sterblichen Reste lösen sich auf, und der Dämon kehrt mit ihren Seelen in die Hölle zurück, um die ewige Folter zu beginnen.

Miles de personas desaparecen a diario. Es obvio que algunas son víctimas de accidentes o asesinatos mientras que otras desaparecen voluntariamente para huir de las circunstancias. Aquí, un demonio del infierno entra en nuestra dimensión, atraído por el aura de gente malvada. Viene a buscarlos, arrancando las cabezas de sus víctimas para que no puedan escapar a la muerte. Sus restos mortales desaparecen y el demonio regresa al infierno con sus almas para dar comienzo a torturas eternas.

Des milliers de personnes disparaissent chaque année. De toute évidence, certaines sont victimes d'accidents ou de meurtres, et d'autres disparaissent volontairement pour diverses raisons qui leur sont propres. Mais il reste d'autres cas... Ici, un démon venu de l'enfer se glisse dans notre dimension, attiré par l'aura des personnes maléfiques. Il vient les chercher, arrachant la tête de ses victimes de façon à ce qu'elles ne puissent simuler la mort. Leur dépouille disparaît, et le démon retourne en enfer avec leurs âmes pour les soumettre à des tortures éternelles.

Devils Dream

An evil entity takes a sinister delight in watching innocent, naked, sacrificial victims torn apart and eaten by packs of hideous monsters. This gruesome and macabre image accurately reflected a passage in the book. The rough was passed by the publishers and the artwork completed. In the end it was considered too risqué for the mass market, highlighting the difference between the author and the artist. The former, using the vehicle of language, can create images that are not ikmmediately apparent; the artist, with his instantly accessible medium, has a far more difficult task when illustrating such subjects.

Un ente maligno se complace en contemplar a víctimas inocentes y desnudas mientras son despedazadas y devoradas por manadas de horribles monstruos. Esta imagen horripilante y macabra reflejaba con precisión un pasaje del libro. Los editores aprobaron el boceto y la obra fue acabada. Al final, la consideraron demasiado atrevida para el mercado y se creyó que destacaba demasiado la diferencia entre el autor y el ilustrador. El primero, por medio del lenguaje, puede crear imágenes que no son inmediatamente aparentes; el segundo, a través de su medio, accesible al instante, se enfrenta a una tarea mucho más complicada al ilustrar tales temas.

Einem bösartigen Wesen bereitet es eine unheimliche Freude zuzusehen, wie unschuldige, nackte Opfer von Horden abscheulicher Monster zerfetzt und aufgefressen werden. Dieses schaurige, makabre Bild bezog sich genau auf eine Stelle des Buches. Der Verleger erhielt den Entwurf, und die Druckvorlage wurde fertiggestellt. Aber dann entschied man, daß es zu gewagt für eine massenweise Vermarktung sei, und man hob den Unterschied zwischen Autor und Künstler hervor. Der Autor, der die Sprache als Ausdrucksform benutzt, kann Bilder schaffen, die nicht sofort offensichtlich sind; für den Künstler ist es dagegen weitaus schwieriger, solche Themen zu illustrieren, da er ein Medium verwendet, das unmittelbar zugänglich ist.

Une entité diabolique prend un plaisir sinistre à contempler le spectacle de victimes innocentes offertes en sacrifice, nues et en larmes, dévorées par des hordes de monstres hideux.
Cette image affreuse et macabre reflète exactement un passage du livre. L'esquisse a été acceptée par l'éditeur, et le travail complété. Mais devant la crudité et le réalisme du dessin définitif, l'éditeur l'a jugé trop risqué pour le grand public. Cet incident met en évidence la différence entre l'écrivain et le dessinateur. Le premier, par les mots, crée des images qui ne sont pas immédiatement apparentes. Le dessin, lui, est instantanément accessible, ce qui rend la tâche des illustrateurs plus délicate lorsqu'ils traitent des sujets comme celui-ci.

The Chair

Gathering cobwebs and dust, a disused electric chair is haunted by the ghost of a vengeful innocent victim. The ghost dwells within the electrical system of the prison, and weird electrical phenomena begin to occur. The executioner of the original victim is lured back to the room, and the electric chair is switched on just one more time...
Compared to the rough, the painting was changed to make the ghost more evil in appearance, and the electric chair more accurately rendered.

Ein stillgelegter elektrischer Stuhl, von Spinnweben und Staub überwuchert, wird vom Geist eines rachsüchtigen, unschuldigen Opfers heimgesucht. Der Geist lebt im Stromnetz des Gefängnisses, und plötzlich ereignen sich seltsame elektrische Phänomene. Der Henker des Opfers wird in den Raum gelockt, und der elektrische Stuhl wird noch einmal eingeschaltet... Das Gemälde entspricht nicht ganz dem Entwurf, da der Geist bösartiger wirken sollte; der elektrische Stuhl ist sorgfältiger wiedergegeben.

Una silla eléctrica en desuso, convertida en un nido de polvo y telas de araña, es frecuentada por el fantasma de una víctima inocente que busca venganza. El fantasma habita en el sistema eléctrico de la prisión y empiezan a ocurrir extraños fenómenos eléctricos. El verdugo de la víctima original se siente atraído hacia el interior de dicha estancia y la silla eléctrica se pone en marcha una última vez...
En comparación con el boceto, la ilustración sufrió cambios con el propósito de hacer el aspecto del fantasma más maligno y de dibujar la silla eléctrica con mayor veracidad.

Couverte de poussière et de toiles d'araignée, une chaise électrique est à l'abandon dans un recoin de la prison. Mais la chaise est hantée par l'esprit vengeur d'un condamné innocent. Le fantôme habite dans le système électrique de la prison, et des phénomènes surnaturels commencent à se produire. Un jour, le bourreau qui a exécuté l'innocent, se sent inexplicablement attiré par la pièce où est entreposée la chaise électrique. Il s'approche, et les manettes s'abaissent une fois de plus...
En comparaison avec l'esquisse, la peinture a été modifiée pour donner au fantôme une expression plus diabolique. La chaise électrique a été rendue avec plus de précision.

Gates of Hell

Planning his latest murder, a serial killer checks aout the suitability of a remote location. He is overcome by the nauseous strench of rotting flesh which becomes so disgustingly powerful and sickly he feels like vomiting. A small sound makes him flick his torch to the doorway. There, two figures stand giggling. With horror he realises that he recognises them. They are two of his formes victims! Sniggering, and with a mocking tone, they tell him "we have come for you - you are ours now"! The adrenalin rushes, his heart thumps in his ears. A scream pierces the darkness– it is his own! That night a man vanished without trace, and his body was never found.

Al planear el siguiente crimen, un asesino en serie se asegura de la adecuación de un lugar remoto. Una pestilencia nauseabunda de carne putrefacta le invade de forma tan poderosa que le produce ganas de vomitar. Un leve ruido le hace encender la linterna y enfocarla hacia el umbral de la puerta. Allí ve dos figuras riéndose. Horrorizado, se da cuenta de que las reconoce.¡Son dos de sus anteriores víctimas! Con tono burlón le dicen: "¡Hemos venido a por ti y ahora eres nuestro!". La adrenalina le sube, oye los latidos de su corazón en los oídos. Un grito perfora la oscuridad: ¡es su propio grito! Esa noche un hombre desapareció sin dejar rastro y su cuerpo nunca fue hallado.

Ein Serienmörder, der seinen letzten Mord plant, besichtigt eine abgelegene Gegend, um zu sehen, ob sie geeignet ist. Ein widerlicher Gestank nach verwesendem Fleisch wird schließlich so stark und ekelhaft, daß er meint, sich übergeben zu müssen. Als er ein leises Geräusch hört, richtet er seine Taschenlampe auf die Tür: da stehen zwei Gestalten und kichern. Voller Entsetzen erkennt er sie wieder: es sind zwei frühere Opfer! Kichernd und in spöttischem Ton erklären sie ihm: "Wir sind gekommen, um dich zu holen. Du gehörst jetzt uns!" Ihm schießt das Adrenalin ins Blut und sein Herz klopft bis zum Hals. Ein Schrei durchdringt die Dunkelheit-er ist es selbst! In dieser Nacht verschwand ein Mann, ohne eine Spur zu hinterlassen, und sein Körper wurde nie wiedergefunden.

A l'issue de son dernier meurtre, un tueur en série voudrait se trouver loin du lieu de son crime. Il se sent prêt à vomir, écœuré et malade, vaincu par la nauséeuse résistance de la chair pourrissante. Un léger bruit lui fait tourner sa torche vers la porte où deux silhouettes apparaissent en ricanant. Le tueur réalise avec horreur qu'il reconnaît ces visages. Ce sont deux de ses premières victimes ! Ricanant d'un ton moqueur, elles lui lancent: "Nous sommes venus pour toi ! Tu es à nous, maintenant !". L'adrénaline se rue le long de ses nerfs, les battements de son cœur l'assourdissent. Un cri déchire les ténèbres: c'est le sien. Cette nuit là, un homme a disparu sans laisser de traces, et son corps n'a jamais été retrouvé.